ENGINEERED BY NATURE

Animal Homes and Hangouts

By Louise and
Richard Spilsbury

BELLWETHER MEDIA • MINNEAPOLIS, MN

Jump into the cockpit and take flight with Pilot books. Your journey will take you on high-energy adventures as you learn about all that is wild, weird, fascinating, and fun!

This edition first published in 2017 by Bellwether Media, Inc.

No part of this publication may be reproduced in whole or in part without written permission of the publisher. For information regarding permission, write to Bellwether Media, Inc., Attention: Permissions Department, 5357 Penn Avenue South, Minneapolis, MN 55419.

Library of Congress Cataloging-in-Publication Data

Names: Spilsbury, Louise, author. | Spilsbury, Richard, 1963- author.
Title: Animal Homes and Hangouts / by Louise and Richard Spilsbury.
Other titles: Pilot (Bellwether Media)
Description: Minneapolis, MN : Bellwether Media, Inc., 2017. | Series: Pilot.
  Engineered by Nature | Audience: Ages 7-13. | Audience: Grades 3 to
  8. | Includes bibliographical references and index.
Identifiers: LCCN 2016034483 (print) | LCCN 2016043522 (ebook) | ISBN
  9781626175860 (hardcover : alk. paper) | ISBN 9781681033150 (ebook)
Subjects: LCSH: Animals–Habitations–Juvenile literature. | Animal
  behavior–Juvenile literature.
Classification: LCC QL756 .S65 2017 (print) | LCC QL756 (ebook) | DDC
  591.56/4–dc23
LC record available at https://lccn.loc.gov/2016034483

Printed in the United States of America, North Mankato, MN.

Table of Contents

Home Sweet Home

Animals are **engineered** by nature to survive in their **habitats**. They use **adaptations**, or features, to build homes and hangouts. These places keep them safe from bad weather and dangerous **predators**. They also give animals a place to rest and raise their young.

Some animals build tall **mounds**. Others dig underground **burrows**. Animals also use materials such as leaves and sticks to make shelters. Some even carry their homes on their backs!

DID YOU KNOW?

Rabbits use their strong legs to dig burrows. If they sense danger, they race inside!

A group of rabbit burrows is called a warren.

5

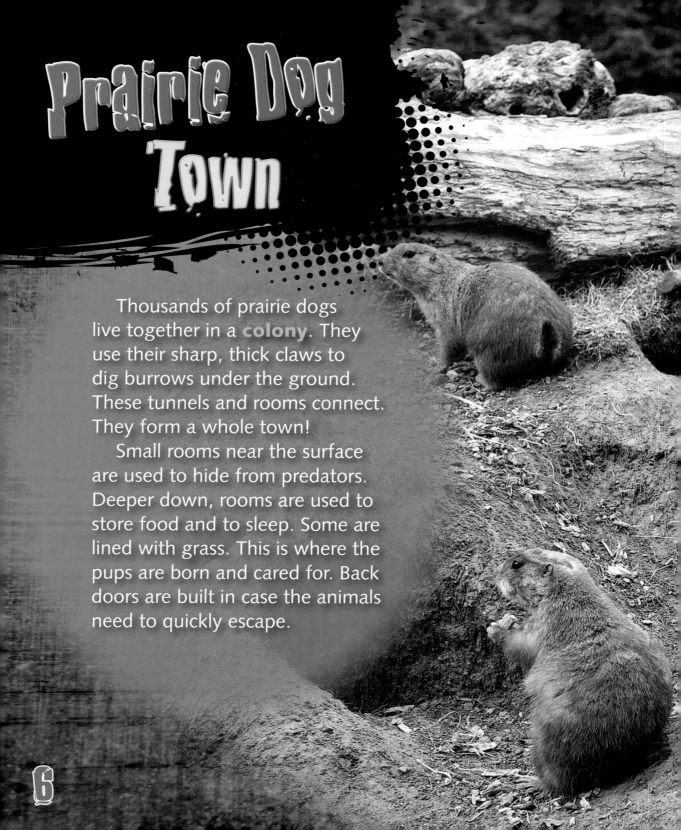

Prairie Dog Town

Thousands of prairie dogs live together in a **colony**. They use their sharp, thick claws to dig burrows under the ground. These tunnels and rooms connect. They form a whole town!

Small rooms near the surface are used to hide from predators. Deeper down, rooms are used to store food and to sleep. Some are lined with grass. This is where the pups are born and cared for. Back doors are built in case the animals need to quickly escape.

The biggest prairie dog towns stretch for hundreds of miles!

DID YOU KNOW?

For lookouts, prairie dogs use mounds built near their burrow entrances. If a predator is spotted, one prairie dog barks a warning. Then everyone rushes inside!

Termite Mound

A single termite is about the size of a grain of rice. But when millions of termites work together, they build enormous mounds!

First, the termites mix soil, spit, and **dung** in their mouths. The termites use this mixture to build layers of walls and tunnels. When it dries, the mixture hardens like cement.

FAST FACT

Termites are always repairing their mounds. Some of these structures are more than 50 years old!

The termites live in a nest beneath the tall mound. Here, they even have a garden where food is grown to eat!

Aardvark Burrow

An aardvark has been feeding on insects all night. But morning is coming, so it is time to dig a burrow!

The aardvark has spoon-shaped claws. It uses these sharp claws and its strong legs to scoop earth out of the ground. While it digs, it squeezes its nostrils shut to keep out dirt.

FAST FACT

Sometimes aardvarks dig larger burrows where their babies are born and raised.

The aardvark finishes digging a burrow almost 10 feet (3 meters) long. It is safe from predators there. The aardvark curls up inside to rest until the next night.

ACTIVITY

Engineering in Practice

The shape of an aardvark's claws helps it dig. See how this works. You will need an old fork and spoon, two plates, and some flour.

- Try using each utensil to move flour from one plate to the other.
- Which shape moves the flour fastest? Why?

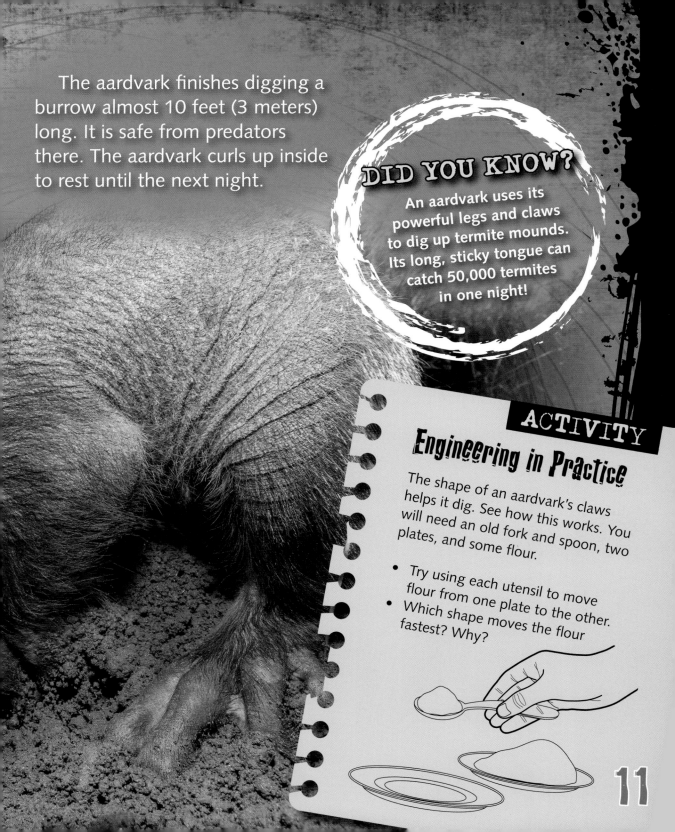

Weaverbird Nest

The male baya weaverbird needs to attract a **mate**. So, he must build an impressive **nest**. To start, he gathers long strips of grass.

First, the bird makes a loop. Then he uses his strong beak to **weave** and knot more grass into a ball-shaped nest. This is where his mate will lay her eggs.

FAST FACT

A weaverbird makes up to 500 trips to gather all the material it needs to build a nest!

The bird weaves a long tube at the bottom of the nest. This narrow, upside-down entrance will keep rain and predators out!

DID YOU KNOW?

Baya weaverbirds will often build their nests hanging over water. This gives it extra protection from hungry animals.

Beehive

The honeybees have found a dark, quiet place to build their hive. It is time to get to work!

The bees bring up **wax** stored in their stomachs. They chew the wax until it is soft. The wax is stuck together to make tiny rooms called cells.

Each cell has six sides. They fit snugly together. The bees build up layers of cells to make **honeycombs**. Together, the honeycombs form the hive.

honeycomb

FAST FACT

Cells in a honeycomb are used to store things such as honey and eggs.

DID YOU KNOW?

Sometimes a hive becomes too crowded. So, some bees fly off to build a new hive. This process is called swarming.

cell

Weaver Ant Nest

A group of weaver ants climbs on to a large leaf. Some of the ants link legs to form a chain across the leaf. They bend the leaf's edges together to make a tent.

Other ants carry **larvae** in their strong jaws. They gently squeeze the larvae as they move along the leaf's edges.

FAST FACT

If an animal attacks a nest, thousands of weaver ants swarm out to defend it!

Squeezing makes the larvae ooze **silk**. The silk works like glue to hold the leaf's edges together. This creates a space for a new nest inside the folded leaf!

Chimpanzee Nest

At dusk, it is time for the chimpanzee to make a nest. First, it climbs high into a tree. It will be safe there. Predators cannot see it from the ground!

DID YOU KNOW?

In the morning, a chimpanzee leaves its nest to find food. It usually builds a new nest each evening.

The chimpanzee bends some large branches. Then it pushes smaller branches between them. It weaves the branches together to make a sort of basket.

Then it puts some leafy branches inside the nest. This makes a comfy bed for the chimpanzee to sleep on!

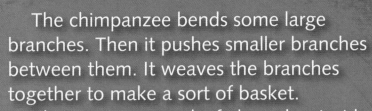

FAST FACT

Chimpanzees choose trees with sturdy branches to build their nests in. That way, they will not fall out!

ACTIVITY

Engineering in Practice

Weaving makes a strong structure. Try it yourself! You will need 12 pipe cleaners, a square of card stock, and tape.

- Lay six pipe cleaners in a row over the square. Leave a little space between each one. Tape the ends down.
- Take the other six pipe cleaners. Weave each pipe cleaner over and under the first layer.
- Remove the tape.
- How strong is your "chimpanzee nest"?

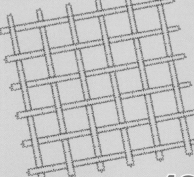

Beaver Lodge

A beaver uses its sharp front teeth to chew through a tree trunk. Boom! The tree falls. The beaver carries it away in its mouth.

The beaver has built up rocks and mud under the water. It uses trunks and branches to build a **dam** on top. The dam blocks the water from flowing in the stream. This creates a calm pond. There, the beaver uses more wood to build a dome-shaped **lodge** to live in.

dam

FAST FACT

Beavers use mud to fill holes between branches and trunks in their dams and lodges.

lodge

Caddisfly Case

A caddisfly larva is in danger. There are many fish in the stream that want to eat it! To protect itself, the larva collects materials from the stream bed. It gathers twigs, sand, and bits of snail shells. It uses its silk to glue the materials to its soft body. This forms a hard, protective case.

The front half of the larva's body sticks out of its case. To hide, the larva just pops inside!

DID YOU KNOW?

When it is time for the larva to turn into an adult, it seals the ends of its case. It breathes through small holes in the case while it changes.

Some caddisfly larvae make cases from tiny rocks mixed with bits of sparkling stones and gems!

case

Engineering in Practice

Mixing materials with a cement or glue-like substance makes a strong structure. Try this cool activity to see for yourself!

- Cut a straw in half.
- Paint one half with glue.
- Roll the straw in bits of sand, sticks, stones, or shells. Let it dry.
- Lay the two halves of the straw side by side. Press down on them.
- Notice how the "case" helps support and protect the straw!

Hermit Crab Shell

To keep safe, a hermit crab does not make a den or burrow. It survives by hiding inside an empty shell left behind by a sea snail or another crab. The shell protects its soft body from animals that try to eat it.

FAST FACT

During a hot day, a hermit crab will burrow into wet sand to cool off.

24

The crab carries the shell wherever it goes. When it grows too big for its shell, the crab just leaves and finds a larger shell to crawl into!

DID YOU KNOW?

When a group of hermit crabs finds a new, large shell, they form a line beside it. The largest crab moves into the new shell. The next largest crab moves into its shell, and so on!

Froghopper Froth

A mother froghopper lays her egg on a plant stem. Soon, a tiny **nymph** hatches!

The nymph sucks in air and blows sticky bubbles from its bottom. This creates a white froth that hides the nymph from predators. It also keeps the nymph from drying out in the sun.

Inside the froth, the nymph sticks its straw-shaped mouth into the plant. It sucks up and feeds on juices from the plant as it grows.

froth

FAST FACT

The froth around a froghopper nymph is sometimes called cuckoo spit.

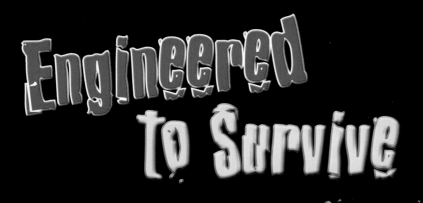

Engineered to Survive

Animals need their homes and hangouts to survive. Prairie dogs run into their burrows to escape hungry predators. A hermit crab is safe and sound inside its hard shell. A weaverbird's upside-down door keeps its nest dry.

FAST FACT

Some bowerbirds mix plant material with spit. This makes a paste that the birds use to paint the walls of their nests!

Aardvarks and chimpanzees rest in their homes after eating. Weaver ants and froghoppers make shelters to keep their eggs safe. One day, all of these animals' babies will grow up and build their own amazing homes and hangouts, too!

DID YOU KNOW?

A male bowerbird doesn't just build a nest. He decorates it, too! He scatters colorful flowers, glass, and stones around his nest to attract a mate.

Glossary

adaptations—features or characteristics that an animal has that help it survive

burrows—holes in the ground

colony—a group of the same kind of animal that lives together

dam—a barrier or wall that stops water from flowing

dung—animal poop

engineered—designed and built

habitats—the natural areas in which organisms live

honeycombs—groups of six-sided cells made of beeswax

larvae—young insects right after they have hatched

lodge—a den built by a beaver

mate—an animal's partner

mounds—piles of hard, packed dirt

nest—a structure that animals live in and raise their young in

nymph—a young insect that has almost the same form as the adult

predators—animals that catch and eat other animals

silk—sticky threads produced by some animals

wax—a substance bees use to make honeycombs

weave—to cross strands of material over and under one another

To Learn More

AT THE LIBRARY

Gray, Leon. *Amazing Animal Engineers*. North Mankato, Minn.: Capstone, 2016.

Scarborough, Kate, and Martin Camm. *A Wasp Builds a Nest: See Inside a Paper Wasp's Nest and Watch It Grow*. Toronto, Canada: Firefly Books, 2016.

Wilkes, Angela. *Discover Science: Animal Homes*. New York, N.Y.: Kingfisher, 2017.

ON THE WEB

Learning more about animal homes and hangouts is as easy as 1, 2, 3.

1. Go to www.factsurfer.com.
2. Enter "animal homes and hangouts" into the search box.
3. Click the "Surf" button and you will see a list of related web sites.

With factsurfer.com, finding more information is just a click away.

31

Index

The images in this book are reproduced through the courtesy of: Glass and Nature/ Shutterstock, front cover, pp. 1, 12–13; Nick Biemans/ Shutterstock, pp. 4–5; Evikka/ Shutterstock, pp. 6–7; Worldswildlifewonders/ Shutterstock, p. 7 (right); PK289/ Shutterstock, p. 8 (right); Offroad Media Productions/ Shutterstock, pp. 8–9; Martin Harvey/ Alamy, pp. 10–11; Tahirs Photography/ Shutterstock, p. 12 (bottom); Debbie Steinhausser/ Shutterstock, pp. 14–15; Shaiith/ Shutterstock, p. 15 (bottom right); Tewan Banditrukkanka/ Shutterstock, pp. 16–17; Danita Delimont/ Alamy, pp. 18–19; Arterra Picture Library/ Alamy, pp. 20–21; Pictureguy/ Shutterstock, p. 21 (bottom); WildPictures/ Alamy, pp. 22–23; JetKat/ Shutterstock, pp. 24–25; Ian Grainger/ Shutterstock, pp. 26–27; Colin J D Stewart/ Shutterstock, p. 27 (bottom); Wildlife GmbH/ Alamy, pp. 28–29.